2004

To Scot

Love

Maureen

I Fiona, fy annwyl chwaer,
gyda chariad O.L.

Acknowledgments
Many prayers in this book were taken from or inspired by
Carmina Gadelica, published by Scottish Academic Press

Text copyright © 2001 Lois Rock
Illustrations copyright © 2001 Amanda Hall

Original edition published in English under the title *Celtic*
Prayers to Guard and Guide You by Lion Publishing plc,
Oxford, England. Copyright © 2001 Lion Publishing plc.

North American Edition published by Good Books, 2001.
All rights reserved.

CELTIC PRAYERS TO GUARD AND GUIDE YOU
Copyright © 2001 by Good Books, Intercourse, PA 17534
International Standard Book Number: 1-56148-335-4
Library of Congress Catalog Card Number: 2001024660

Library of Congress Cataloging-in-Publication Data

   Celtic prayers to guard and guide you / written and
compiled by Lois Rock ; illustrated by Amanda Hall.
      p. cm.
   ISBN 1-56148-335-4
   1. Prayers. 2. Celtic Church--Prayer-books and devotions--
English. 3. Hymns, Scottish Gaelic--Translations into English.
4. Incantations, Scottish Gaelic--Translations into English. 5.
Christian poetry, Scottish Gaelic--Translations into English. I.
Title.
BV245.R62 2001
242'.8'0089916--dc21   2001024660

Celtic Prayers
to Guard and Guide You

Written and compiled by Lois Rock
Illustrated by Amanda Hall

Intercourse, PA 17534 • 800/762-7171 • www.goodbks.com

Introduction

For hundreds of years, the Celtic peoples have lived on the rugged westerly shores of Britain and France. They have known the fierceness of stormy seas and wild weather, and the beauty of pastures growing green under clear blue skies. They have known the uncertainty of life in a world that is beautiful, puzzling and sometimes threatening.

Celtic Christians believe in a God who has made everything, both sunshine and storm, and they turn to God for help and protection in all the details of everyday life. Their traditional prayers, handed down through the generations, ask simply and earnestly for God's blessing: that God will guard us, guide us and do good things for us through all our days.

Each day be glad to thee,
No day be sad to thee,
Life rich and satisfying.

From *Carmina Gadelica*

May God's goodness be yours,
And well and seven times well
May you spend your lives.

From *Carmina Gadelica*

Our God is the God of all,
The God of heaven and earth,
Of the sea and the rivers;
The God of the sun and of the moon
and of all the stars;
The God of the lofty mountains
and of the lowly valleys,
He has His dwelling around heaven
and earth, and sea, and all that in them is.

St Patrick

God to enfold me,
God to surround me,
God in my speaking,
God in my thinking.

God in my sleeping,
God in my waking,
God in my watching,
God in my hoping.

From *Carmina Gadelica*

May the white-winged angels
Encircle thee around.
May they guide thy footsteps
Upon the holy ground.

Thine be the might of river,
Of earth and sea and sky.
Thine be the might of rushing wind,
The might from God on high.

Walk the way of kindness,
Walk the way of right,
Walk the way of wisdom,
Walk the way of light.

Traveling moorland, traveling townland,
Traveling mossland long and wide,
God the Son about your feet,
Gold-bright angels at your side.

May God make safe to you each steep,
May God make open to you each pass,
May God make clear to you each road,
And may He take you in the clasp of His
own two hands.

From *Carmina Gadelica*

Delightful I think it to be
   in the bosom of an isle
on the crest of a rock,
that I may see often
the calm of the sea.

That I may see its heavy waves
over the glittering ocean
as they chant a melody
   to their Father
on their eternal course.

That I may bless the Lord
who has power over all,
heaven with its crystal orders
   of angels,
earth, ebb, flood-tide.

St Columba at Iona

God bless the house from roof to ground,
With love encircle it around.
God bless each window, bless each door,
Be Thou our home for evermore.

O God of the weak,
O God of the lowly,
O God of the righteous,
O shield of homesteads:

O may I find rest everlasting
In the home of Thy Trinity,
In the Paradise of the godly,
In the Sun-garden of Thy love.

From *Carmina Gadelica*

I take the seed, I go to sow
In name of Him who makes it grow.
I breathe the wind that blows so soft
And throw a handful high aloft.
Where the rock is hard and bare
No plant will sprout, no flower be there.
Where the seed falls to the soil
A harvest will reward my toil.

Harvest of leaf,
Harvest of fruit,
Harvest of stem,
Harvest of root;
Harvest of lowland,
Harvest of hill,
Harvest that all
May eat their fill.

Each meal beneath my roof,
They will all be mixed together,
In name of God the Son,
Who gave them growth.

Milk, and eggs, and butter,
The good produce of our own flock,
There shall be no dearth in our land,
Nor in our dwelling.

From *Carmina Gadelica*

Peace between neighbors,
Peace between kindred,
Peace between lovers,
In love of the King of life.

Peace between person and person,
Peace between wife and husband,
Peace between woman and children,
The peace of Christ above all peace.

From *Carmina Gadelica*

The peace of joys,
The peace of lights,
The peace of days,
The peace of nights.

Be Thou between me and all things grisly,
Be Thou between me and all things mean,
Be Thou between me and all things gruesome,
Coming so darkly, coming unseen.

I will not lie down with evil,
Nor shall evil lie down with me,
But I will lie down with God,
And God will lie down with me.

From *Carmina Gadelica*

God be with us
On this Thy day,
Amen.
God be with us
On this Thy night,
Amen.
To us and with us,
On this Thy day,
Amen.
To us and with us,
On this Thy night,
Amen.

From *Carmina Gadelica*

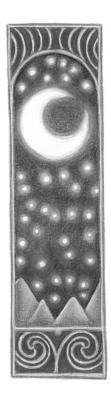

Each shade and light,
Each day and night,
Each time in kindness,
Give Thou us Thy Spirit.

From *Carmina Gadelica*

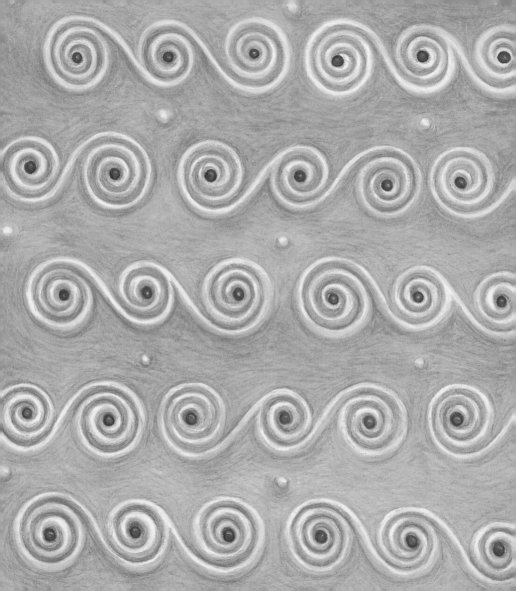